ARGYLL'S LODGING

&

MAR'S WARK - STIRLING

Doreen Grove and Richard Fawcett
Principal Inspectors of Ancient Monuments

CONTENTS

Edited by Chris Tabraham
Designed by Ramsay Gillies Design
Photography by David Henrie and Mike Brooks,
Historic Scotland's Photographic Unit
Illustrations by David Simon
Published by HISTORIC SCOTLAND

First published 2002
Printed in Scotland from sustainable material by
Howie & Seath Ltd., Edinburgh
ISBN 1 903570 40 9

HISTORIC SCOTLAND

A Tour of Argyll's Lodging

On entering the courtyard of Argyll's Lodging the visitor quickly forms the impression that the house exudes an air of timeless architectural unity. However, the gentle pink harling conceals a complex building history.

1

1. The house began life in the mid sixteenth century, when John Traill built a two storeyed house in the north-east corner.

2. Later that century Adam Erskine expanded the house upwards and outwards, adding two more storeys to Traill's house, a short wing to its south, and a little later a kitchen wing to its west, so creating an L-shaped tower house. The courtyard was probably already enclosed, and contained stables and other buildings, even at this stage. It is difficult to detect this sixteenth-century building because of the subsequent changes.

2

3

3. The purchase of the house in 1629 by Sir William Alexander began its metamorphosis from the chrysalis of an unexceptional tower house to the extraordinary butterfly we see today. Sir William extended the existing short wing of the tower house southwards, to form an imposing range containing a suite of principal rooms. At its south end a further short range returned to the west to balance the main body of the earlier house. This created an elegant house ranged around a courtyard and screened from the street by a wall. Both the interior and exterior of the building were lavishly decorated.

This tour guides the visitor around the house, highlighting the important features. It begins in the ground-floor rooms of the south wing, where there is an introductory display about the house and its owners. Thereafter it progresses through the sequence of rooms forming the principal apartment, before finally returning to the courtyard.

Modern craftspeople have recreated the furniture and furnishings listed in two inventories made of the contents, in 1680 and 1682, as faithfully as possible, to help us to experience how the principal rooms in the house functioned.

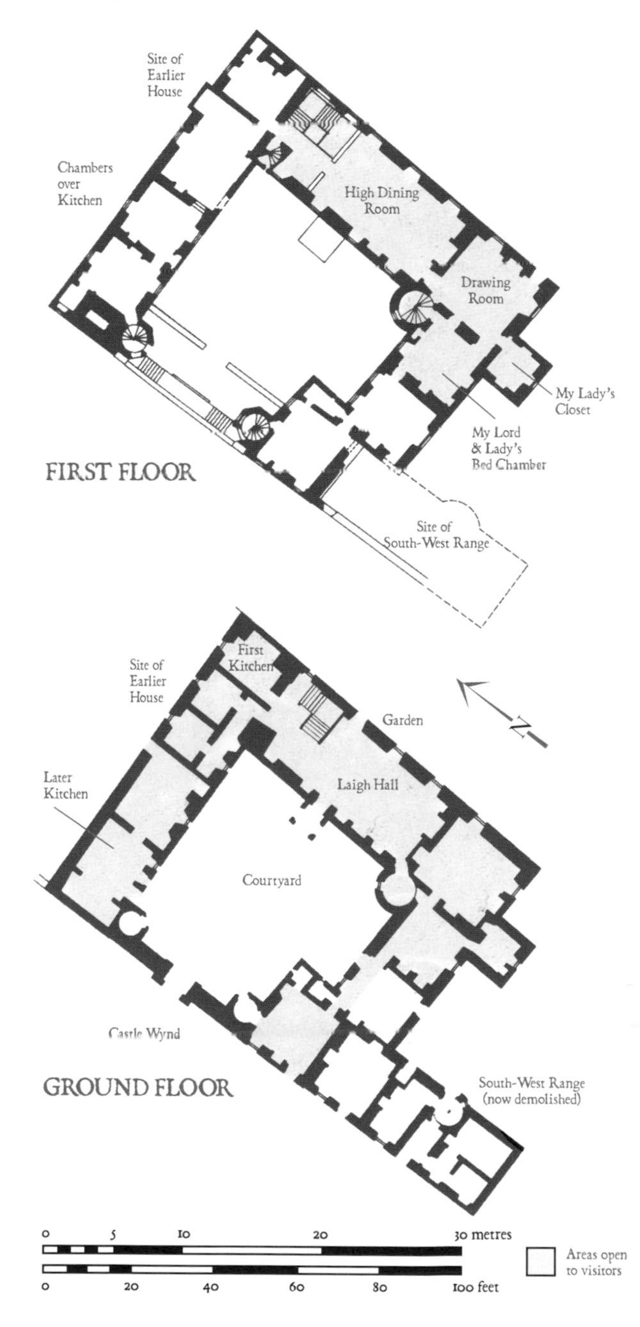

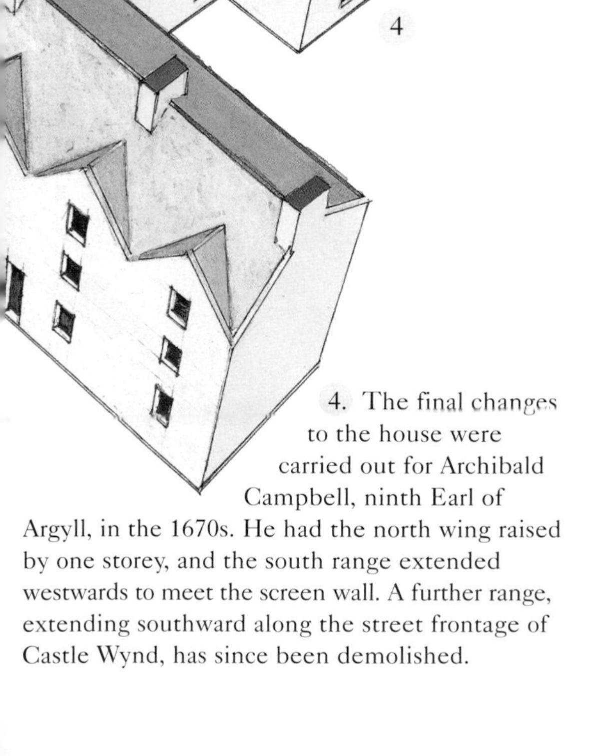

4. The final changes to the house were carried out for Archibald Campbell, ninth Earl of Argyll, in the 1670s. He had the north wing raised by one storey, and the south range extended westwards to meet the screen wall. A further range, extending southward along the street frontage of Castle Wynd, has since been demolished.

'BELOW STAIRS'

The principal rooms of Argyll's Lodging were on the first floor (*piano nobile* or noble floor). 'Below Stairs' was mainly used for service accommodation and by the servants.

The South Range

The master of the household, the earl's steward, may have occupied the room that is now the souvenir shop, whilst beyond it was a suite of two rooms and a closet (described as 'the room within') that Archibald, Lord Lorn, the earl's eldest son, occupied. The room in the south-east corner was known as the lower dining room, and contained two tables, with a carpet on each, and 20 rush and leather chairs.

There was also a 'woman house', or laundry room, in this part of the house. The laundry room was more than simply a place to wash clothes; here the female servants cleaned, starched, ironed and mended, as well as made fine white linen shirts and undergarments for the household. It was fitted out with 'stent trees' (clotheshorses) and 'lint wheeils' (spinning wheels).

The Laigh Hall

From the south range we enter the 'laigh hall' ('laigh' is Scots for 'lower'). Had we been visiting the Earl of Argyll in 1680, we would have entered this room direct from the courtyard through the main west door.

In the 1680s the laigh hall was simply furnished, with one long table and fire irons for the decorated fireplace. It served as an entrance hall and also perhaps as the main dining hall for the earl's senior household servants.

The Laigh Hall.

The Main Stair

The splendid main stair at the north end of the laigh hall lies within the area of the earlier tower house. It was formerly separated from the laigh hall by a screen. There were five 'back' stairs in addition to the main stair – two spiral stairs at the inner angles of the courtyard, two further spiral stairs in the octagonal turrets at the outer angles of the courtyard, and a fifth spiral stair behind the street range. These made it possible for each apartment, or suite of rooms, to be separately accessed.

A door to the right of the main stair opens out onto the gardens. These pleasure grounds were once extensive but are now considerably reduced in extent. The ninth Earl of Argyll was a keen gardener and had several terraces laid out with formal parterres and walks.

The Main Stair.

The Kitchens

The three cellars through the door at the north end of the laigh hall are within the basement of the earliest part of the house. At the east end is a kitchen, with an arched fireplace and a domed bread oven to one side. This was either the 'little kitchen' or the 'baikhouse' in 1680. To the west are two more cellars, an ale cellar and a brewhouse. Since brewing and baking both involved yeast the two operations were usually carried out close to each other.

Beyond these again are the pantry and the great kitchen. Both were provided in the 1680s with tables for preparation, water tubs, a salt basket, pans, stewing dishes, spits for cooking and two great iron grates as well as dozens of plates and trenchers for serving the food.

Most of the food prepared in these kitchens was supplied from the earl's estates; with much of the county of Argyll as his larder it is unlikely that there would have been many shortages. Because of the difficulties of storing and transporting fresh food, smoking and salting were common ways of preserving meat and fish. It is also likely that some food at least arrived on its own four feet, to be slaughtered and butchered here in Stirling.

The Great Kitchen.

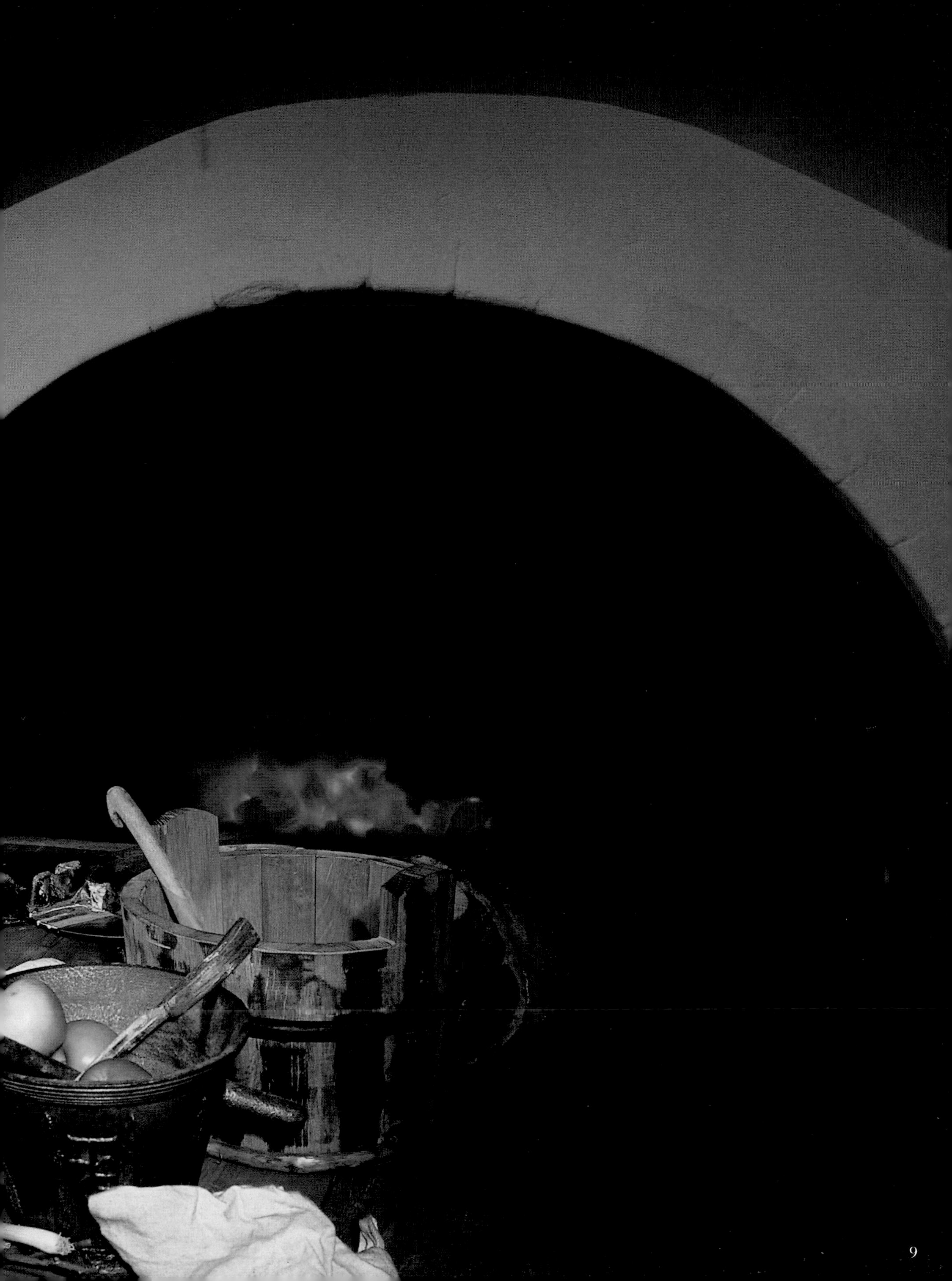

'Above Stairs'

Ascending the main stair, we enter the most important rooms of the house, those reserved for the Earl and Countess of Argyll's own use.

The High Dining Room

The high dining room was the principal reception room in the house. It is entered from the main stair through an imposing doorway, its pediment decorated with the earl's initials and a coronet.

Here the owners entertained their guests in fine style. It was sumptuously decorated in the latest fashion by David McBeath, an Edinburgh artist, in 1675. We can see the finest example of his work on the wooden partition separating the room from the stair. The design consists of 19 Corinthian pilasters between the dado, or chair rail, and the ceiling frieze and cornice.

Decorative unity was given to the room by the painted frieze reflecting the carved decoration on the existing fireplace, itself a feature dating to Lord Stirling's time of the 1630s.

The panels between the pilasters were used to display the family's collection of paintings. In 1682 the room held portraits of the earl and his countess, Lady Sophia Lindsay (the countess's daughter by her first marriage) and the Earl of Seafield (the countess's father), as well as a painting of a ship, a seascape and a still-life of grapes.

The furniture in 1682 included 12 folding tables and 30 chairs covered with a yellow stamped material called 'druggit'. During dinner these would have been arranged in various combinations in the centre of the room, then moved to the side when not in use or if the guests wished to dance.

The High Dining Room, and (top left) David McBeath's painted decoration on the partition wall. Elsewhere only small areas of the decoration have survived, and in order to protect the original work the design has been copied onto modern lining paper. The entrance doorway (top right) from the main stair has the earl's initials and coronet in the pediment overhead.

Earl of Argyll's chair of e in the Drawing Room) and (below) the room's ndid fireplace, a legacy n Lord Stirling's time in 1630s.

The Drawing Room

When alone or entertaining honoured guests, the earl and countess withdrew into their private, or state apartments. The first of these was the drawing room, a smaller but altogether more sumptuous room than the high dining room. The walls were hung with five pieces of tapestry, serving to demonstrate the richness of the decoration as well as providing warmth and draught proofing. The earl sat upon his chair of state with 'twa pein of purpur stamped stuff courtains with an cover for the seat of the same', while his family and guests sat on cane or 'wand chairs' only half of which had 'carpet cushions'.

The room also contained a clock, a finely inlaid cabinet topped with crystal vases for flowers, a fir table, a looking glass and a little carpet - and for entertainment 'ane fyne harp'.

The splendid fireplace is decorated with mythical beasts and the arms of Lord Stirling and his wife, Lady Janet Erskine. Immediately to its right, behind a tapestry, is a doorway (now blocked) that once led to a timber gallery overlooking the formal gardens. Evidence for the gallery was discovered in the stonework, beneath the harling, during recent repair work to the exterior of the house.

My Lady's Closet

Perhaps the most remarkable room in the whole house was the small chamber entered off the drawing room, 'my Lady's closet'. In 1680 the list of furnishings and precious objects in this room is longer than for any room except the wardrobe, or storeroom. It also gives us an unusual insight into the personality, preoccupations and delights of Lady Anna Mackenzie, the ninth earl's second wife. In addition, the fact that the list is so reduced by the date of the second inventory, two years later, points to Lady Anna's very special loyalty to her husband in his exile abroad - she possibly disposed of her own treasures to support him.

In 1680 the furnishings consisted of a writing desk, provided with an ink horn, a small table covered with a cloth of stamped purple, five cane chairs, a chest of drawers, small sweet wood (possibly cedar) boxes and candle-sticks. There was also a variety of glass bottles, porcelain dishes and a pestle and mortar, presumably for mixing medicines or cosmetics. This room was where the countess kept her most treasured possessions - several small statues, portraits of her husband and of Mr Baxter, a minister whose preaching she particularly admired, a Cambridge Bible (edited to remove the sections proscribed by Acts of Parliament), silver tumblers and gilded cutlery. Rather more prosaically, the small room was provided with a bell for summoning servants, fire irons and a 'closed stool', or toilet box. Two years later virtually all that remained were the hangings, the chest of drawers, a few chairs and the good Reverend's portrait.

My Lord and Lady's Bedchamber

The final room in the sequence is 'my Lord and Lady's bedchamber'. Although it was undoubtedly the most private of the suite of rooms, even this was used for entertaining, though only for the most privileged guests. Indeed, the earl or countess may have received their guests while sitting up in bed, dressed in their finest raiment, as a sign of aristocratic condescension. No visitor could have failed to be impressed by the richness of the furnishings, particularly the great bed with its purple stamped curtains and bed cover, matching wall hangings and closed stool. In addition, there were two looking-glasses, a chest of drawers, a cabinet and seven chairs.

Because there were no corridors within this part of the house, all the rooms interconnected. Behind the hangings to the right of the fireplace is a doorway that led through to other family rooms (it was blocked up when Argyll's Lodging became a military hospital in the nineteenth century). Another sign of change within the chamber is the blocked-up window also in this wall, to the left of the fireplace, a reminder that this was once the full extent of the Earl of Stirling's house.

The Courtyard

Returning to the front entrance it is worth pausing in the courtyard to observe the architectural finesse and apparent unity of the building. We have seen that the house developed in four main stages (see pages 4-5). The work of the first two was entirely subsumed within the expansion of the house, firstly by Lord Stirling, then by the ninth Earl of Argyll. Externally, the house was lavishly adorned; even the bases of the chimney stacks were elaborated with scrolls, or volutes. The corners of Lord Stirling's buildings have buckle-shaped quoins, a common motif in the 1630s, and it is the position of these on the south elevation of the courtyard that gives the clearest indication of the extent of his house. The windows, particularly the dormers, have elaborate strapwork gablets.

At this date only the upper parts of the windows were glazed, whilst behind were two levels of shutters; the present sash and case windows were installed during the building's use as a military hospital. Whoever designed Lord Stirling's house was a master-mason of high calibre. Stirling's second son, Anthony, appointed joint royal master of works in 1629, may have been involved. But as the architecture has close affinity with major contemporary buildings, such as Heriot's Hospital in Edinburgh, the master-mason here could have been either William Ayton, in charge of the building work at Heriot's for a time, or perhaps John Myln, a later royal master of works. Both men were involved in building Cowane's Hospital in Stirling in the same decade.

The Earl of Argyll heightened the north wing, completed the south wing and built or remodelled the range that ran along the street front of Castle Wynd (since demolished).

Although the detailing of Argyll's additions is more restrained than Lord Stirling's, the decoration of the outer gate to the screen wall, with its massively rusticated Tuscan pilasters and arch, is probably his handiwork. The windows and doorways are capped by pediments of segmental or concave triangular form, some bearing an earl's coronet and the boar's head crest of the Argylls; one doorway pediment is dated 1674.

Yet the distinction between the work of the two noblemen is not straightforward. Window pediments on the first floor of the north wing are identical to those on Argyll's south wing but they bear the initials of Lord Stirling and his lady. The doorway at the base of the stair turret at the outer end of that wing, identical to the turret at the outer end of the south wing dated 1674, has traces of the date 1633. However, it seems unlikely that the upper floors and stair turret of the north wing in their present form were part of Lord Stirling's work. Although we cannot be sure, it seems that Argyll was recording his own contribution along one side of the courtyard and that of his predecessor along the other. Given the close links between the two families, this perhaps comes as no surprise, and may be seen as recognition by Argyll of the work of his predecessor.

The buckle-shaped quoins along the south range show the extent of Lord Stirling's building.

The courtyard from the outer gate (far left), and (inset) Lord Stirling's coat of arms above the main entrance. The Earl of Argyll's outer gate (left) with its Tuscan design, was perhaps inspired by an engraving by Alessandro Francini, published in Italy in 1631 but which only became available in English in 1669.

The Story of Argyll's Lodging

The mighty landholding magnates who played a leading role in the government of medieval and early modern Scotland depended on royal favour for their prosperity. In return for their land they were obliged to undertake considerable duties on behalf of the Crown. These included attending the royal court from time to time, and wherever their sovereign chose to reside.

From the twelfth century Stirling Castle was one of the most important of these royal residences. When the royals were there, some of their principal courtiers were accommodated therein also. Others would have had to find lodgings in the burgh. However, as ideas of what was fitting for a nobleman expanded, most of the great families came to see the attraction of building a town house for their own convenience.

Argyll's Lodging, formerly the residence of the Earls of Argyll, is now the finest and most complete surviving example of a seventeenth-century aristocratic town house in Scotland.

The Earl and Countess of Argyll arrive at their Stirling town house in 1680; an artist's impression by David Simon.

Broad Street, Stirling, around 1800. Mar's Wark graces the far end. (Courtesy of the Smith Art Gallery and Museum, Stirling.)

The First Town House

The main approach to Stirling Castle passed through the market place, in what is now Broad Street. This area and the wynds around it came to be flanked by fine houses of the nobility and the wealthier burgesses. The Campbells of Argyll owned various tenements within Stirling from at least the fourteenth century. By 1600 this included the corner plot where Broad Street met Castle Wynd. Sir William Alexander, whose family was closely connected to the Campbells, acquired the adjacent property on Castle Wynd in 1629.

It is not clear who built the house that Sir William subsequently bought and extended. It may well have been John Traill, a wealthy burgess of St Andrews, who sold it in 1559 to Adam Erskine, commendator (lay administrator) of Cambuskenneth Abbey. Erskine in turn passed it to a relative in 1604. It is perhaps significant that Sir William Alexander was married to Janet Erskine at the time he purchased the house from a branch of his wife's family; indeed, it appears that most of the changes of ownership here were between kin or closely related families.

Lord Stirling's Contribution

Sir William Alexander was born around 1577 at Menstrie, the family seat held of the Earls of Argyll, north-east of Stirling. He became a prolific poet, writing many of his odes on royal themes. He was very highly thought of; indeed, a contemporary, Drummond of Hawthornden, thought his love poetry as good as Shakespeare's!

Sir William soon became a colourful character at the royal court. It may have been Argyll who introduced him. Once there, his career blossomed. He became tutor to the then heir to the throne, Prince Henry, and in 1603, at the Union of the Crowns, followed his sovereign to London. He was knighted in 1609, made Secretary for Scotland in 1626 and created Viscount Stirling in 1630.

Sir William Alexander, Lord Stirling (c. 1577-1640)

Sir William spent much of his life dreaming up 'get rich quick' schemes, most of which failed spectacularly. By far his most ambitious scheme was the attempted colonisation of Nova Scotia following a grant of the territory in 1621. Alexander sold 6000-acre parcels of land, along with the honour of a baronetcy. The scheme eventually lost royal support and collapsed.

The prospect that Charles I (1625-49) would return home to Scotland for his coronation brought with it the hope of a regular royal presence in his northern kingdom. Alexander decided to improve his new town house in Stirling. When the king finally arrived in 1633, Alexander was further ennobled as Earl of Stirling and Viscount Canada. But despite his rich and varied life, his financial ineptitude saw him die insolvent in 1640. His town house he left to his fifth son, Charles, but the Town Council soon foreclosed on a mortgage they held on the property. For a time they proposed to turn it into an almshouse but the scheme was abandoned in the 1660s when the Earl of Argyll agreed to buy it.

The fireplace in the High Dining Room (top), a legacy from Lord Stirling's time, and (right) a window gablet overlooking the courtyard bearing the date 1632.

Argyll's Lodging

Archibald Campbell, ninth Earl of Argyll, was born in 1629. His father is best remembered for his Covenanting sympathies and his conflict with the royalist Marquis of Montrose in the Civil War of the 1640s, for which he paid with his life in 1661 shortly after Charles returned from exile.

The young Archibald, more strongly royalist than his father, succeeded in having the family estates and earldom restored to him. He befriended the Secretary for Scotland, the Duke of Lauderdale. Their families became close, Argyll's sister marrying the duke, his son the duke's stepdaughter, and his daughter, Anne, the duke's eldest nephew and heir. Archibald, while still Lord Lorn, had married Lady Mary Stewart, daughter of the Earl of Moray, in 1649. Lady Mary died in 1668 shortly after giving birth to their thirteenth child!

By now Lauderdale was trying to persuade the king to return to Scotland and rebuild his palaces. The possibility of court life returning to Stirling may have been the stimulus for Argyll to extend and embellish his residence in the 1670s. Charles did not return, though his rather troublesome, and overtly Catholic, brother, James, Duke of Albany, did in 1681, as High Commissioner to the Parliament. He visited Argyll at his lodgings in Stirling that same year.

'The last sleep of Argyll' by E.M. Ward (1857). The painting hangs in Edinburgh Castle, where the ninth Earl of Argyll spent his last night on God's Earth.

Unlike Lauderdale, James was less than impressed with his host, concerned about his strong Protestantism and the scale of his power and influence. The turning point in Argyll's life came in the same year with the Test Act. This demanded that all office holders recognise the sovereign as supreme in spiritual as well as temporal matters. Argyll prevaricated, was imprisoned in Edinburgh Castle, tried for treason and condemned to death. He escaped to Holland by dressing up as the maid of his stepdaughter, Sophia, who had come to visit him.

Paradoxically, these troubled years are the reason we know so much about the fixtures and fittings of Argyll's Lodging. The earl's feeling of insecurity led him to have inventories taken of the house in order to pass the house and its contents to his second wife, Lady Anna Mackenzie, daughter of the Earl of Seafield, whom he had married in 1670. Lady Anna was the widow of the Earl of Balcarres and had several children by her first marriage. During her second husband's exile, the countess spent most of her time in Stirling. Argyll's lands were declared forfeit and she survived for a while using the income from an estate granted to her by her first husband. King Charles eventually granted her a pension as a personal favour because of her first husband's loyal support.

The death of Charles and the accession of his brother as James VII in 1685 brought with it outright rebellion. Argyll led a rising in Scotland to coincide with one in England headed by the Duke of Monmouth. The earl struggled to raise an army and in June he was captured near Renfrew and summarily beheaded under the sentence passed on him in 1681. Like his father, in his days before his execution, he wrote letters to his family from his prison cell in Edinburgh Castle; his own serenity was passed on in letters of comfort to his wife and family.

Argyll's Lodging from Castle Wynd.

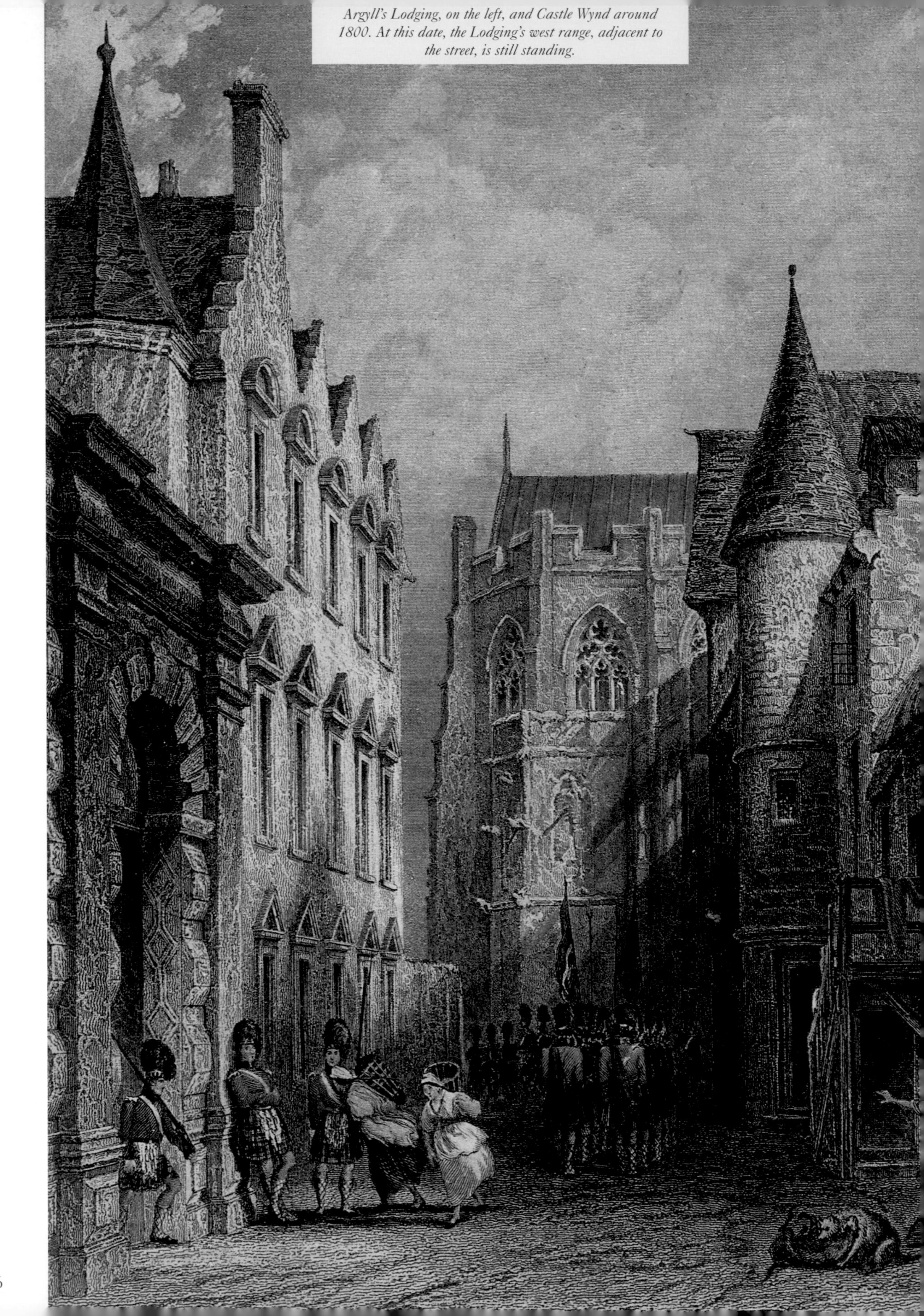
Argyll's Lodging, on the left, and Castle Wynd around 1800. At this date, the Lodging's west range, adjacent to the street, is still standing.

A Military Hospital

Argyll's Lodging remained in the Campbells' possession for over a century more. Payments were made for repairs to Adam Jack, slater, John Ferguson, smith, and Alexander Howie, glazier, in 1706. The Duke of Cumberland, George II's son, stayed in the house in 1746 during his campaign to crush the Jacobite Rising. In 1764 the fourth Duke of Argyll sold the house to Robert Campbell and James Wright, who in turn sold it on to the McGregors of Balhaldie. During this period the west range facing Castle Wynd was demolished. Around 1800 the army bought the building for use as a military hospital.

Although Stirling Castle had long held soldiers, it was not until the eighteenth century, when the army increased in size to provide troops to supply the ever-expanding empire, that the ancient fortress became a major army barracks. During the Napoleonic Wars, the army grew six-fold, from 40,000 to 225,000 men, putting great pressure on garrisons like Stirling. The chapel royal, great hall and palace were all converted for military use. At the same time the army recognised that the small infirmary in the 'king's old building' in the castle was also woefully inadequate; hence the purchase of Argyll's Lodging.

For over 150 years, Argyll's Lodging served as a military hospital, longer perhaps than it had served as an aristocratic town house.

The building was well suited, with several large rooms capable of housing wards, and sufficient smaller rooms for use as surgeries, dispensaries, stores and staff accommodation for surgeons, a chaplain, medical staff and sergeants.

The use the rooms were put to over the years varied, as did the number of staff and patients. The top floor provided wards, patients' dining room and staff accommodation, the first floor more wards, an ablutions block, further staff accommodation and significant storage space (my lord and lady's bed chamber became the linen store), and the ground floor kitchens, surgeries and medical offices, including a mortuary in the souvenir shop! Fortunately for history, the army made little impact on the building, for although the windows were altered to the present sash-and-case ones, most of the original doors and fireplaces survived. The army finally vacated the building in 1964 when Stirling Castle ceased to be a military depot.

Argyll's Lodging then became a youth hostel. In 1996 Historic Scotland opened the main rooms to visitors, using replica furnishings to display them as they may have looked when the ninth Earl of Argyll and his Countess played out the rather sad days of the early 1680s.

Argyll's Lodging in the 1950s, shortly before it passed out of use as a military hospital.

The Inventories

Two inventories of the fixtures and furnishings of Argyll's Lodging were made, in 1680 and 1682. Each is described as: *Ane Inventor of all the furniture In the Earle of Argyl his lodging at Stirling Subt by the sd Earle and Anna Countes of Argyll*, and seems to have been specifically drawn up to enable the earl to transfer the ownership of his house and its contents to his wife and family.

Twenty-seven rooms with their furniture and fittings are listed, starting in the attics and working their way down to the ground floor. They provide a wonderful insight into the objects that were deemed of value and therefore worth recording. The wardrobe in the attic (in those days a wardrobe was a room rather than a piece of furniture) has by far the longest list, including a considerable quantity of the furnishings and fabrics then in store.

It is hard for us to imagine the value of fabric in the seventeenth century; importation of rich foreign fabrics was restricted and subject to punishing import taxes; the domestic industry was unmechanised and unpredictable and the production of clothes and furnishings was expensive and time-consuming. The Campbells were fortunate in being able to afford to keep a tailor in their Stirling residence. He made outdoor clothes and probably some of the soft furnishings for the house. Even in the grandest house, fabrics from both garments and household furnishings were recycled for re-use. All the linen and undergarments were manufactured at home, most likely by the women servants; but the ladies of the house may also have done fine 'white work'. We see evidence of this in the 1682 inventory in the objects listed in the 'woman house'.

A table setting in the High Dining Room. Modern craftspeople have recreated the furniture and furnishings listed in the inventories as faithfully as possible, to help visitors experience how the principal rooms in the house were furnished.

Of the 27 rooms identified, all but the important public rooms were provided with bedsteads. This is presumably an indication of the number of servants and staff that were accommodated within the house. Privacy in those days was viewed altogether differently. Each suite of rooms had additional beds for maids or servants, some rooms had several box beds with mattresses stuffed with chaff and plain 'stuff' covers, while one bed is described as a folding bed. So, although the inventory only names two members of the earl's staff - the tailor and the master of the household - it is clear from the number of beds (17 in all) that there were a considerable number of servants living in the house. Throughout the house several of the chambers (not just bedchambers) are provided with closed stools, not unlike modern chemical toilets. Primitive as this may seem to us, such stools had only become fashionable in the houses of the nobility earlier that century.

The rooms beyond 'my Lord and Lady's bedchamber' are now inaccessible, but the 1680 inventory gives us some information about their uses. The attic floor contained some family rooms, while the remainder was used as storage (the 'wardrobe') and as the tailor's workroom. In addition to the earl and countess, several other members of the family had suites of two or three rooms each, although it is not quite clear where these were located. Lady Jean, the earl's 19-year-old daughter, had a room and two closets, the outer one containing a bedstead, presumably for her maid. Lady Sophia Lindsay, the countess's daughter from her first marriage, also had a suite of three rooms; she had married her stepbrother Charles, the earl's fourth son, in 1678. She is listed as having a sitting room, bedchamber and chamber 'within', also supplied with a bedstead, again perhaps for her maid. Lord Lorn, the earl's eldest son and heir - in 1680 a 22-year-old married man - had a three-roomed suite, all with beds, but only his own had a 'closed stool'.

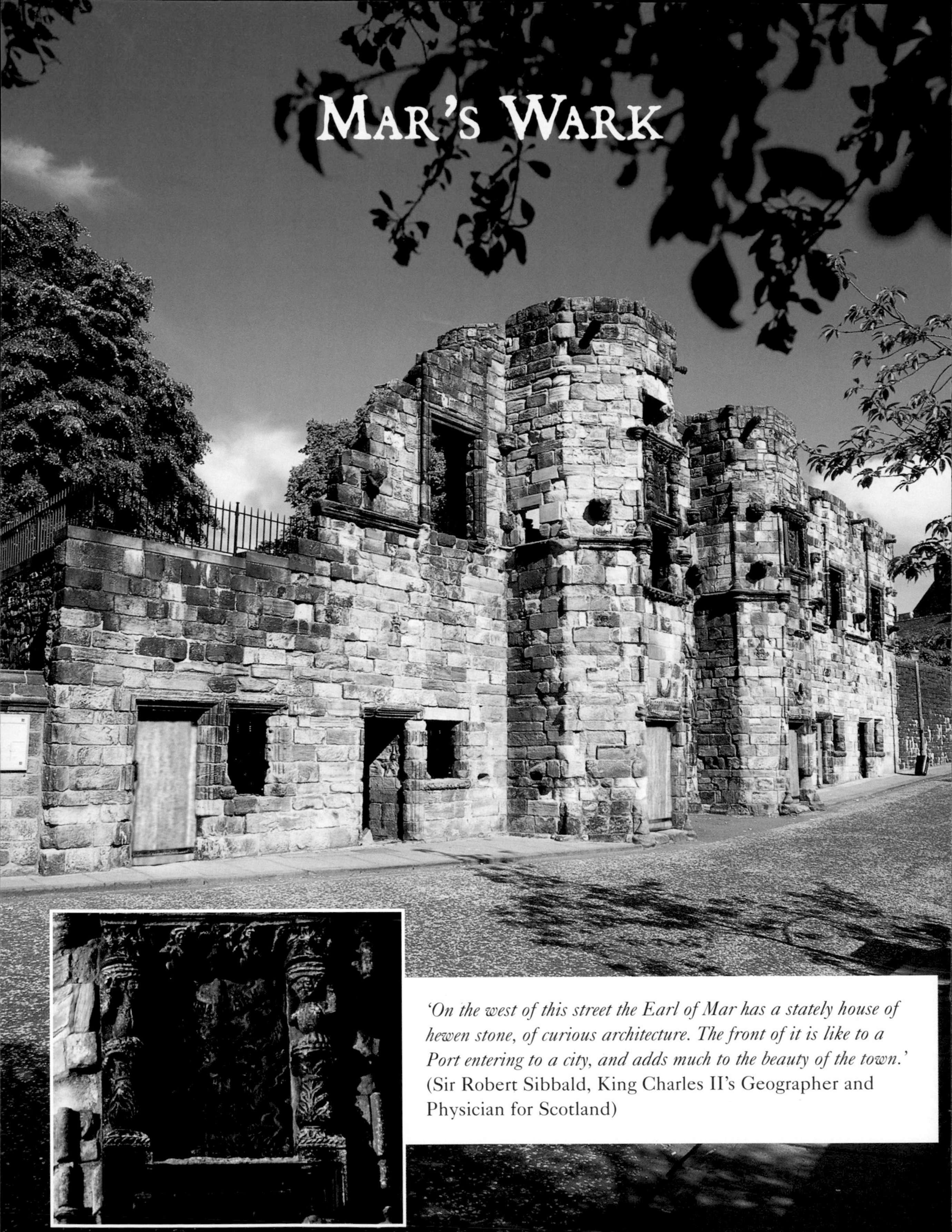

Mar's Wark

'On the west of this street the Earl of Mar has a stately house of hewen stone, of curious architecture. The front of it is like to a Port entering to a city, and adds much to the beauty of the town.'
(Sir Robert Sibbald, King Charles II's Geographer and Physician for Scotland)

John Erskine, Earl of Mar

John Erskine (c.1510-72), the first Erskine Earl of Mar and hereditary keeper of Stirling Castle, chose one of the most prominent sites in the burgh of Stirling for his new town house - the top of Broad Street, adjacent to the parish church of the Holy Rude and on the wynd leading to the castle. Dated stones and documentary records indicate that building work was largely completed by 1570, though the original scheme was never finished.

John Erskine had an eventful career spanning two reigns. During most of Mary Queen of Scots' personal reign he served as keeper of mighty Edinburgh Castle, and in 1565 was rewarded with the earldom of Mar. Two years later he was removed from Edinburgh Castle, but by way of compensation was granted the hereditary keepership of Stirling Castle, an office many an Erskine before had held on a non-hereditary basis. It became a position of particular importance after the queen's abdication later the same year, for Mar also had custody of the young James VI. Mar probably began to plan his new house in Stirling - Mar's Wark - around this time. With the family's main residence at Alloa a few miles away, it was clearly important to him to have another close by the royal castle of which he was keeper.

Mar certainly had the wherewithal to build something grand for at the Reformation the Erskines had acquired control of three monasteries - Cambuskenneth, Inchmahome and Dryburgh. Not only did these provide a handsome income, but there is also a tradition that Cambuskenneth was robbed to provide the building stone! Several fragments of ecclesiastical stone, including an incised consecration cross, can be seen re-used in Mar's Wark.

Mar attained the height of his power in his dotage. From September 1571 until his death at Stirling Castle in October of the following year, he was Regent of Scotland. George Buchanan, the king's tutor, describes how Mar, at his accession, tried to 'break through the guarded streets to the market place and at last ordered a body of his musketeers to occupy his new house, which was nearly finished and overlooked the whole market place'.

Mar's period as regent was dominated by the man destined to replace him, James Douglas, Earl of Morton. Morton frustrated every effort made by Mar to achieve peace, hastening his end. Buchanan described the regent 'finding his pious endeavours for peace thwarted, worn out with the vexations and cares of public life' retiring to Stirling 'where he died, as was generally supposed of a broken heart'.

Mar's Wark wasn't long in following its master into decline. The departure of King James for London in 1603, following the Union of the Crowns, saw the departure also of the second earl south. The use of Mar's Wark, never more than intermittent, became even more so now. After the earl's death in 1634, Lady Marie spent her remaining years in dispute with her stepson, the third earl, and whilst she occupied rooms in Stirling Castle, the third earl and his countess occupied Mar's Wark and the family's main Alloa residence. Thereafter, Mar's Wark was little used by the family. In 1733 Stirling Town Council approached the Erskines with a view to turning Mar's Wark into a workhouse. The idea came to nothing. Despite efforts to have the building demolished, it survived, and in 1907 the 'venerated ruin and invaluable historic landmark' passed into State care.

Mar's Wark (far left), and (inset) the Earl of Mar's coat of arms on the south tower. The Earl of Mar's portrait (left) copied by John Scougall after an unknown artist is courtesy of The Scottish National Portrait Gallery.

The main facade of Mar's W[...] and (inset) examples of it[...] sumptuous carved decorati[...]

Mar's Wark

The Earl of Mar intended his town house to form a quadrangle around a courtyard. Although all that remains is the main facade overlooking Broad Street, it is clear both from the building and eighteenth-century drawings that there were ranges around two other sides of the quadrangle. Whether the fourth side was ever enclosed is unclear.

Despite the decay, the splendour of the main façade is still stunningly obvious. When built, the street frontage was about 35 m long. At its centre was an arched **entrance gateway**. The pend, or passage, that once led through to the courtyard has a fine transverse-ribbed segmental vault, and in its north wall an arched recess, no doubt for a porter's bench. Semi-octagonal **towers** flank the gateway, each provided with its own door and a pistol-hole overlooking the main entrance.

On each side of the gateway are vaulted **basements**, nine in all. As well as providing a secure platform for the main rooms overhead, most of the vaults were entered separately from the street through a door and lit by a single window. They were probably shops, an arrangement not inconsistent with a grand town house. Across Europe can be found town houses of comparable scale combining commercial and private accommodation.

The elegant façade represents something of the best of the Renaissance in Scotland. The main source of architectural inspiration for the detail is easily found at James V's palace in Stirling Castle, built 30 years earlier. The arrangement is regular and well balanced, and wonderfully embellished with nook-shafts at every corner and good figurative carving that repays closer inspection. These comprise heraldic and inscribed panels, human and animal masks, dummy gargoyles (water spouts) and statuettes, including a curious statue of a female corpse apparently wrapped in a winding sheet immediately to the right of the right-hand tower (*see top left*). The sculpture affords us a peep into the world inhabited by the stonemasons who created them. All the windows were half-glazed, shuttered and fitted with iron grilles to improve the security of the house.

The north tower door gives access to two vaulted chambers, while the southern door once gave access up a circular stair to the upper floors. A spacious **reception hall** formerly occupied much of the first floor. It was well lit by the windows overlooking Broad Street and there is evidence for a canopied fireplace between the central window and the stair tower. The west wall is almost entirely missing, so any arrangement between the hall and the south range or the stair in the south-west corner of the hall is now lost. A wall once separated the hall from a smaller room to the north (a slight stub of the wall can be detected between the two most northerly windows). This room also had a fine canopied fireplace in its north wall and may have served as a **withdrawing room** off the great hall. How this chamber connected to the north range is now a mystery, like so much of the story of Mar's Wark.

Prominently positioned above the arched entrance gateway is a **heraldic panel** containing the royal arms. The heraldic panels on the adjacent towers depict the Earl of Mar's arms - those on the south tower his own, and those on the north tower impaled with those of his wife, Lady Annabella Murray of Tullibardine. The door lintels were inscribed with couplets. The north one reads:
THE MOIR I STAND ON
OPPIN HITHT MY FAVLTIS
MOIR SVBIECT AR TO
SITHT,
('The more I stand on open height my faults more subject are to sight')

and the south one (*see right*):
I PRAY AL LVIKARIS ON
THIS LVGING
VITH GENTIL E TO GIF
THAIR IVGING
('I pray all lookers on this lodging with gentle eye to give their judging')

The viewers' judgement can only have been highly favourable.

FURTHER READING

On the Lodgings:

J Ronald *The Earl of Mar's Lodging, Stirling* (1905)

J Ronald *The Story of the Argyle Lodging* (1906)

Royal Commission on the Ancient and Historical Monuments of Scotland *Inventory of Stirlingshire, vol 2* (1963)

C McKean *Stirling and the Trossachs* (1985)

Richard Fawcett *Stirling Castle* (1996)

On the Noble Families:

A Lindsay *A Memoir of Lady Anna Mackenzie* (1868)

J Willcock *A Scots Earl: the Life and Times of Archibald Ninth Earl of Argyll* (1907)

T McGrail *Sir William Alexander, First Earl of Stirling* (1940)

Argyll's Lodging, by Robert Billings, c.1845.
Front cover: The Drawing Room, Argyll's Lodging.